It's Still
Lion vs Christian
in the Corporate Arena

It's Still
Lion vs Christian
in the Corporate Arena

Wally Armbruster

CONCORDIA®

Publishing House
St. Louis

Library of Congress Cataloging in Publication Data

Armbruster, Wally.
    It's still lion vs Christian in the corporate arena.

        1. Christian life—1960-   2. Business
ethics.   I. Title.
BV4501.2.A65   248'.88   78-31394
ISBN 0-570-03791-3

TO JACK
TO ME
And
TO ALL LEO-CHRISTIANS*

*There isn't much point in your reading this book if you aren't a Leo-Christian: someone who aggressively seeks to be successful in business (a Lion) but also wants to be successful as a follower of Jesus (a Christian). If you are . . . you probably are within what a marketing plan would call my "target audience."**

(**Insidious term, isn't it?)

Contents

It's my style to write books like this to myself.

What I do is force myself to think about things that I'd rather not listen to: things that disquiet me. Or challenge me. Or frighten me.

I certainly don't look forward to facing the questions I'm going to have to ask myself on *this* subject, because I've made a lot of money and reached the lofty position of (Wow!) executive vice-president of a Big Company in the Corporate Arena.

Come along if you dare. Or care.

I promise to listen if you will.

W.A.A.

Preface

The Gladiators' Entrance to the Arena

It was Jesus Christ—though it could have been a business man—who stated the obvious principle: "You cannot serve two masters."

When you accept a job in a corporation, you are expected to dedicate yourself to it totally. But suppose you have already made another commitment—to Christ—whose demands are equally absolute: "He who loses his life for My sake will find it"; "He who is not with Me is against Me"; "He who loves father and mother [or boss or company] more than Me is not worthy of Me." That comes even closer to total commitment.

So what do you do as a committed Christian in a corporation? Scratch off any business job as out of bounds—leave business in the hands of people who are totally dedicated to it? Or find some way to be *both* a dedicated Christian and a dedicated executive?

If Jesus is right—and your commitment to Him says you believe He is—you are to be *in* the world but not *of* the world. He is counting on you as a committed Christian to stay in the world of business—not to conform to its sometimes unethical practices, but to transform it by serving Him *through* your job. If business is ever to change in the direction of the values you believe are eternal and best for business, then only people like you will be able to influence it with a dedication equal to that of the dedicated corporate person.

All right—assume you've opted to enter the corporate arena as a committed Christ person. You feel He deserves your first and final loyalty. After all, who else has died for you and brought you into a forgiven relationship with God Himself, who will be around long after the Fortune 500 have disintegrated?

Assumption number two: You've been blessed with desirable business skills and experience. You get a job in a corporation. Now what happens?

You're unmistakably in a dangerous situation. You will quickly encounter ready-made conflicts between you and certain contrary principles. You will be strongly tempted to abandon or set aside your commitment to Christ in favor of corporate approval and advancement. Or you will creatively attempt to find ways to be both a good Christian and a good member of the corporate team.

In a word—you will be reliving the struggle of Wally Armbruster—a committed Christian who is still trying to be a valuable corporate executive—bringing the positive, human, and fair values of the Ten Commandments into the corporate arena.

Here's Wally, a valiant fighter, taking a breather from the tournament to visit his dressing room. Don't be shocked at the blood on these pages. It's a do-or-die struggle. But he thinks it's worth the effort. He wouldn't be in it if he didn't love the business world and its potential for good. As he wins, the corporation wins.

With people like Wally—and you—in it, the corporate arena can be a glorious place.

—The Publisher

11

1

Lion vs Christian

The title of this book might suggest that I regard the Corporate Arena as a battlefield for the Bad Guys vs the Good Guys.

I don't.

Nor do I restrict the real meaning of the Corporate Arena to the Fortune 500. If you're a holier-than-thou goodygoodnik, drooling at the prospect of a book that categorically condemns big business to hell, I'm sorry to disappoint you. My meaning of the term includes any organization (small business, social, religious, family, labor union, recreational, or educational) in which either success or security offers challenges to a Christian's Christianity.

The title of this book is not Lions vs Christians (plural); it's Lion vs Christian (singular).

I really don't think there *is* a conscious battle of

LIONS
(with goals and methods so success-and-profit-oriented that they are openly and defiantly antichristian)

vs

CHRISTIANS
(with goals and methods so heaven-oriented that they are openly and defiantly anti-Lion).

13

My purpose in writing this book is to have the guts to examine . . . and perhaps expose . . . the conflicts which can occur between me-the-Lion (the aggressive seeker of success/profit/security) and me-the-Christian (who would like to be just as aggressive in my pursuit of living up to the Ten Commandments and to the Beatitudes).

You might say it's a matter of principle vs principal. (But then again, you might not because that's a pretty rotten pun.)

I really do want to be both a successful Lion and a successful Christian. I assume that you do, too. So I have coined a new word to describe us and to make it easier to refer to us throughout this book:

Leo-Christians.

For Leo-Christians, the part of life that offers the most challenges to Christian commitment is also the part that offers the most opportunities to fulfill that commitment. And that part of life is nine to five, payday to payday.

This applies mightily to hierarchy Leo-Christians (the corporation V.P., the department head, the school principal, the foreman, the archbishop). But I think I can show that it's also applicable to den mother, clerk, secretary, middle manager, customer, production line worker, or kindergarten teacher . . . or anyone else who has a role to play on what Shakespeare called the stage, the world we live in. And it's precisely those roles we play that cause most of the conflict of Lion vs Christian . . . within oneself or between two parties in a situation or between an individual and the "organization."

Primarily, though, I'll be talking about business. About businessmen and businesswomen in America . . . in the Corporate Arena.

And since this is the introductory chapter, I want

14

to introduce myself as a fierce friend of business, businessmen, and free enterprise. I can really get ticked off at people who take sweeping potshots at business—big business, especially.

Most of the business people I've met—yes, even big wheels like presidents and chairmen of the board of Fortune 500 companies—are ethical, charitable, hard-working, dedicated, church-going people who (contrary to the bad-mouthers and Naders) really do *not* conspire to shaft the public.

They want very much to produce good products at fair prices. Fair, however, to both consumers and their stockholders; they feel responsibility to both, and that takes delicate balance.

I have seen them exhibit real concern for employee morale. And I have seen them openly *enjoy* sharing profits, giving salary increases and promotions to those who deserved them.

They donate a whale of a lot of time and money to the community. It's a real sacrifice for them to attend those boring, chicken-and-peas fund-raising dinners after working hours (with no pay) when they'd rather be home watching Monday Night Football or reading a book.

Sometimes I hear employees of a company—even the middle managers and those near the top—refer to their company's "management" or "the corporation" as if it were either:

some faceless, personless, insidious "thing" located "somewhere" that "somehow" runs the company . . .

or

three powerful, ruthless, Mafia-like monsters-in-business-suits who have henchmen to carry out their orders and make offers you can't refuse.

Actually, in my experience, the people at the *very*

top of most companies are the brightest, easiest-to-reason-with, most responsible people in the whole company. They are usually very warm, friendly people who want very much to be recognized as individuals. Far from being antichrists, they openly declare for God. They love their families and want desperately to *be loved* by everybody . . . but especially by their own employees. They dream of being loved even by their customers. Honestly, I mean that.

They knock themselves out to do a good job. They want to deserve their role. Most work so hard and such long hours—10 to 12 hours a day—I simply can't understand how they have gotten such a rotten reputation for "living the life of Riley" or "spending half their time on the golf course." Even the ones who "inherited" the presidency of their companies work those hard and long hours. But an awful lot of those big shots started out as little shots . . . started at the bottom and worked their way to the top, as proud of America as they are of themselves because it still is a place where that is *possible.*

Are they lawbreakers? Of course not. And they don't stay out of jail merely because they have good company lawyers to keep them out. I think 99 percent would tell you, honestly, that they would not even *consider* doing anything illegal. They would consider the question insulting—not only to their morality but also to their sanity.

Are they unethical? With almost the same degree of incredulity (but perhaps with even greater vehemence) they'd tell you that they NEVER violate professional ethics. And, in my experience, big businessmen really *do* make every effort to uphold high ethical standards of doing business.

Of course, a lot of books on this subject use the

word "ethics" differently than I use it. A Ph.D. in ethics or theology or sociology uses the word pretty much as a synonym for personal morals . . . to be judged by oneself. In *business,* what's "ethical" or "unethical" isn't simply an individual determination; it's a standard set by and judged by your peers, your competitors, a lot of times by your industry's "association." There are written and unwritten codes of ethics for the AMA, the NAM, the AAAA, the PGA, the ANA, the ADA and just about any other letters you want to string together. Even the Main Street Businessmen's Association has a say-so about what's ethical or unethical for a member to do. And if the members get too sloppy or greedy—if they let their profession's ethics slip too far—the government will step in and declare the heretofore "ethical action" or at least "accepted practice" a clearly *illegal* action. I could cite 50 such developments . . . especially since pollution, cancer, tort liability, and forced recall of faulty products became matters of great concern and cost. And so could you.

Today it's stupid for a businessman to be unethical. It's just not good business. You might have gotten away with it a few years ago, but today the rules are clearly defined, and if you break the rules— ZAP! Either your competitors or some consumer organization or the government will nail you.

Are they immoral? Ah, here's where it gets sticky.

First of all, we must ask: Who's to decide what's immoral and what isn't? I can make moral judgments for only one person: me. And you can make them only for you. And neither of us should make them for anyone else.

What somebody else thinks is perfectly okay may be okay for him. But not necessarily for me.

And the difference is not merely a question of Christian morality vs some other kind of morality. Nor will you find the answers to what I'm talking about in the Ten Commandments.

I'm talking about conducting my business life— every minute of it—according to what I believe *Christ* expects of me. According to *His* interpretation of the Ten Commandments, according to the Beatitudes, according to all those nearly *impossible* standards of living—and loving—He is quoted as having said in the Scriptures.

There are times when I think our only hope is that Matthew, Mark, Luke, and John misquoted him. I mean, *some* of those things He expects are *hard*.

If I understand what Jesus expects, it's not only the avoidance of sin in business, but also to act as He would act. And that, my friend, is a heavy load to carry up the Corporate Ladder.

Sometimes I think: "Boy, Jesus, I wish you had worked for the Bethlehem Steel Company or for Nazareth Industries, Inc., and tried to live up to that love-thy-competitor, wash-the-feet-of-the-office-boy stuff of yours! You never would have made vice-president with that kind of approach!"

I really don't think it's difficult for a Leo-Christian to be legal.

It's not hard to be ethical by Wall Street or Main Street standards.

But it can be tough to live up to everything that's expected of me as a Christian.

It's not much of a struggle on Sunday—unless you're a pro football player. Or too rabid a fan! It's even within the realm of possibility in your role as Christian-Father, Christian-Husband, Christian-Neighbor, or Christian-Citizen.

But any *Leo-Christian* worthy of the name has *got* to have a "decent" amount of "competitive spirit" . . . "fierce pride in his company" . . . "profit incentive" . . . "ambition" . . . right?

And that can pose real problems. If . . .

If we think about it.

What I suspect is that we don't. That "good, loving, charitable, dedicated" Leo I described earlier could be kidding himself.

Let's force ourselves (writing and reading this book) to think about it. We can call it by a business term: taking inventory.

I've separated the discussion of possible conflict into chapters based somewhat on the Ten Commandments and somewhat on the teachings of Christ (as I hear them; it's up to you to decide whether you hear them the same way).

If I read Jesus right, He expects a lot more of us than we have been expecting of ourselves.

And that could (literally) make one hell of a difference!

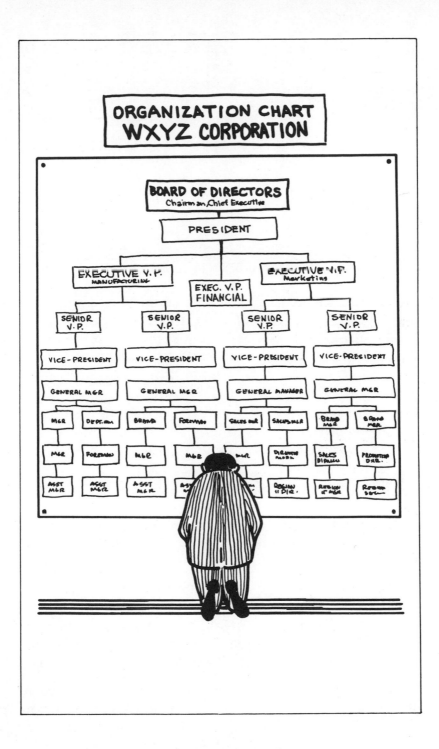

God
vs
The Almighty Corporation

On the surface, I can't imagine anyone admitting that he puts God second or third in his hierarchy.

Reading the Bible, it's hard even to imagine how those Hebrews with Moses could have idolized golden calves and other dumb objects. But apparently they did—because God had to spell it out on a tablet, "Hey, keep your priorities in order. It's O.K. to look at those things as works of art, but when you make gods out of them . . . gods you put ahead of Me . . . that's going too far!"

Twenty centuries A.D there's a chance that we're still doing it. Maybe not stone idols but trophies nevertheless . . . gods like status, fame, sales goals, profit, job security, the corporation, or even the Super Bowl . . . ahead of God.

Oh, stop that! (the Leo in me protests, as he shall in this kind of type throughout the rest of this book). Don't go to extremes. I might want those things very much but it's going too far to accuse me of regarding them as GODS. After all, I don't "worship" them!

Maybe; maybe not. It all depends on what your definition of worship is. It all depends on what you are willing to "sacrifice" to one god or another . . . in a given circumstance.

Well, get specific. Give me some examples of what I do that could possibly qualify as a "sacrifice" to one of these gods?

We'll get into that in pretty fine detail a little later on in this book.

But first, let's consider how intensely we seek those things I mentioned and why it's possible that they have become "other gods."

If we regularly—or even ever—put business considerations ahead of God considerations, that comes dangerously close to constituting a sin against the First Commandment, doesn't it?

Now wait a minute! Ecclesiastes says there is a time for work and a time for . . .

Yeah, but if you read the whole thing I think you'll find the message that God stays consistent about being God and I interpret that as meaning that we should stay consistent in being His followers. But—even sticking strictly to your point about time— I've got to admit that I spend a LOT more time seeking business successes than I do seeking success as a Christian. I can go nine to five, Monday through Friday, without giving God a thought. I NEVER do that to business—not even when I'm on vacation!

As a world at large, we're pretty swept up in business and our occupation. We have gotten carried away with the IMPORTANCE of what we do for a living and how successful we have become at it.

At a cocktail party:

Donald Trieman, UCLA sociologist who has done 10 years of research on the subject, says: "Occupation is easily the chief criterion in determining society's pecking order—not only in industrialized nations

like the US but even among primitive tribes of Southeast Asia and South America."

Business pervades us. And corporations demand that it does.

At the executive or potential-executive level, many corporations don't just employ YOU; if you're a man, they "hire" your wife and family, too. Some actually interview the man's wife . . . or at least ask him plenty of questions to assure that the prospective "executive employee" has a spouse who will "cooperate with the corporate goals" and "participate" in social/business functions and be ready to accept a transfer or anything else that will be "for the good of the company and her husband's career."

And almost all corporations expect a loyalty and dedication which amounts to a religious devotion to your job. They may deny that they expect you to put the corporation ahead of your family; but there is plenty of evidence that the man who regularly declines to come to a Saturday meeting or a business dinner because he has a family picnic to attend or a child to help with homework is quickly tabbed as "having no future with the organization." And try turning down a transfer and promotion because your family prefers to stay put.

Jesus once said, "Render to Caesar the things that are Caesar's and to God the things that are God's." Today He'd have to add, "And render to the corporation the things that are the corporation's."

Now hold on! Family is one thing but no corporation expects you to serve IT before God!

Officially, maybe not. But if you'd like to test it, try mentioning God in the middle of a business discussion and watch what funny looks you get. Try saying, "I disapprove of marketing this new product because it appeals to people's prurient interests and is therefore unchristian" . . . or "We shouldn't have this Christmas sale because it exploits a holy occasion" . . . or "We shouldn't bury this as a business expense because that would be a sin." You can guess how far you will get.

The book *On-the-Job Ethics* (Cameron P. Hall, ed.) quotes a lot of people who frankly admit that the Leo-Christian conflict is severe and that the Leo wins most of the time. One person put it bluntly, "You simply can't do business by Christian principles and survive."

Wow! I wouldn't go that far. But I do think you have to be sensible about it. Sometimes you do have to compromise or look the other way. After all, if you have a family to support and . . .

Sure, it's tough. It's asking a lot. In my case, He might have asked too much. But the easy way out is to blame it on "them"—the guys who run the corporation, the union, the decision-makers.

After all, I didn't make the rules!

No, and we didn't make the Golden Rule either. It's simply a matter of which piper . . . er, uh . . . which god . . . we choose to follow. The

CHOICE is a matter of putting one ahead of the other . . . a god before God.

And not just for the corporate rules-setters but also for the followers. Is it okay to "look the other way," to "carry out an order," to pass on the "little white lie": the cheating way of entering an accounting item to achieve a corporate tax advantage; covering up a boss's perq; padding sales figures in a publicity release to make your company look better, etc.—because to do otherwise would put your job in jeopardy?

I know what you're saying but look, man, this is business. It's a tough racket. You do what you have to do.

I guess that's the point. And so it becomes a decision of who we will sacrifice to . . . the organization god or the Other One.

I've heard the Organization Man described as "that frightening symbol of elastic ethics and compromise." I could describe him as a Leo-Christian who is more afraid of losing his job or his place on the Corporate Ladder than he is of losing his soul. But I'm not insensitive to his dilemma. It ain't easy.

You simply can't follow the same principles in business that you do in your neighborhood or family situations. I'm just a clerk or a secretary or a worker or a vice-president. Now if I were RUNNING this company, I'd . . .

That suggests that we're all victims of those Bad Men at the Top. (Yes, I say MEN because it's still almost exclusively male up there; I didn't say I approve of that situation, so don't attack me, Gloria. I would be delighted to see more women at the top, just to see if they would do it differently and better.)

I think it's baloney to blame the Men at the Top for making a god of the Almighty Corporation.

I blame all of us.

When I say, "The corporation demands such-and-such" I mean that WE demand it of ourselves. It's like mob hysteria. We get caught up in it. We fan each other's fire. If the corporate chief executive did not demand it of us, WE would demand that he did. Or demand that he be replaced by someone who would. The football coach must demand victory of his players because the alumni demand it of the coach. Even when the coach is a "fine builder of character," if he LOSES—whether at Notre Dame or Texas Christian or Secular U.—he is OUT!

And anyway, let's face it: Competition is fun. Winning is a blast. Losing is lousy.

Now you're talking! Rah! Rah! and right on!

It's only human. The positive aspects of corporate dedication and personal success are the crux (hmmm . . . now that's an interesting word in this context, isn't it?) of the matter.

If you have the corporate attitude and ambition, you will be rewarded.

More money. An impressive title. A bigger office. Two philodendron plants instead of one. Perhaps a country club membership and invitations to the boss's house, with wives (as our ornaments). I recognize that that parenthetical sarcasm is not nice. But it's important. So, though I apologize, I decided not to edit it out.

Those symbols of progress are heady stuff. Heady, too, is actual progress in your work and business advancement. You get not only the recognition (having your name appear on the same list of invitees to a meeting as the president's name . . . or at least the sales manager's) but you also get the real satisfaction of having a voice in corporate strategy and decisions. It is both a Leo opportunity and a Christian opportunity—and that's why it's important that you DO advance.

Up there you begin to feel the awe in the air. And perhaps begin to smell that intoxicating incense, the POWER that comes with progress.

Suddenly you can actually SEE the corporate ladder, rung by rung. Count 'em: you, Al, Tom, Mr. Smith, Mr. Gotrocks, and finally, C.B. himself.

And perhaps you begin to covet.

Stop that! That is merely ambition, which is GOOD. Especially since two or three of those guys are either inadequate or over the hill and therefore ripe for replacement. If you play your cards right . . .

Shhhhh! The sales manager is talking about the Competition. "We can DO it, men. They're vulnerable if we hit 'em where they're weak and hit 'em hard. We MUST, repeat, MUST, reach that sales goal we have set and it's THEIR share of the market we must penetrate. We CANNOT be satisfied until we are Number One—because, of course, we deserve it!"

You begin to feel the adrenalin flow. Sure, it's war. Sure, it's them-against-us. Sure, it's dog-eat-dog.

And, man, isn't it fun? Can you deny that?

No, I can't. I admit it. I love it. There's a real thrill in going head-to-head for somebody's business and winning. Even if you don't win, the struggle itself is fun. The getting prepared. The plotting. The dramatization of our strengths and our competitor's weaknesses. The overtime huddles with your team-mates in smoke-filled rooms as the deadline approaches. The smell of sweat from white-shirt

31

warriors smitten with a common cause, the brass ring of victory within our grasp . . .

That, too, is heady, human stuff.

It's not just in business. Missionaries must feel it in competition vs Voodoo . . . Protestant minister vs Catholic priest in competition for a convert in city ghetto or rich suburbia . . . Girl Scouts vs Campfire Girls . . . union vs management . . . my child vs your child . . . even my painting vs your painting or my hotel room vs yours.

It may start out as no problem. But then the desire to win becomes more insistent; you begin to compromise "a little." And soon, a lot. Because it becomes necessary . . . to DO WHAT YOU HAVE TO DO . . . to get elected and stay elected. I really don't think Watergate was a pre-conceived game-plan; it just grew. The sin of Watergate (if I may call it that and I know I shouldn't because that indicates that I'm standing in judgment) isn't terrifying because of specific criminal acts. To me, what's frightening is that STAYING IN POWER can become such a god.

And so can keeping your job, moving up in the organization, getting that increase in wages, reaching that sales goal. Watergates don't happen just on Pennsylvania Avenue. They also happen on Main Street, Wall Street, Produce Row, Tin Pan Alley, the Great White Way, Campus Lane, and Rural Route #1. Wherever there is drive.

It's competition: for money, for power, for prestige, for glory, for winning-for-the-sake-of-winning . . .

Knock it off! It's also for betterment and improvement. And how can we know we're getting better at anything if there isn't some way to tell? To keep score? Victories vs losses? Last year's profits vs next year's profits? March/1979 vs March/1980 sales in "A" markets?

Yes. Consider the plight of the born millionaire. Or even the self-made one. Why on earth would he continue to work? After all, he knows he's going to have to give most of it to Uncle Sam; and he can buy anything he wants.

Well, for one thing, there's the joy of competition and the laurel wreath of victory. He doesn't need the money per se BUT IT'S THE WAY THE WORLD KEEPS SCORE.

And so he seeks more corporate profits and more personal wealth as fiercely as the starving man seeks food or the drug addict seeks a fix or the alcoholic seeks a drink or the saint seeks heaven . . .

Whoa! Not necessarily. I remember when I was very young, I had the gall to ask my boss (who was a multimillionaire) why on earth he continued to work. And fortunately for me he was a kind and understanding man. He looked at me, almost embarrassed to be so good-intentioned and said: "Well, son, for one reason, because of people like you. You have a great deal of talent. Somebody has to have enough capital to run a business to provide the opportunity for young people like you to use and develop that talent— and get paid for it. In this case, that somebody is me. But I enjoy it. That's enough—those two reasons—for me to continue to work."

I agree that it does come down to your motivation. But when there are two motivations which CLASH . . . that's the problem.

We can be motivated by ideals, by idylls, or by idols.

But calling it IDOLATRY . . . isn't that really overstating it?

Believe me, I've tried rationalizing myself out of it. But when business pursuits stop being just something you'd like to have and start becoming something you NEED, you're not far from getting on your knees ... not far from bowing to business considerations even if they conflict with God considerations.

And I thought idolatry went out with the Old Testament.

No. I think, for most of us, idolatry is still a very real possibility.

Good Ol' Number One

Maslow taught us about the basic needs of Man.

First, we must satisfy our basic biological needs—food, shelter, clothing to keep warm. And a Stage 1 Leo-Christian—though driven by his animal instinct and need to stay alive—needn't normally do unchristian acts to satisfy his most basic needs.

Then, when your biological needs are satisfied, you need to keep it that way—to have security. Keep your job, home, car, etc.—or keep the husband or dad who can provide that security.

But then we need something quite different. We then seek fulfillment of our social needs. To have others accept us, recognize us, love us, praise us, regard us as "somebody." This really is a multi-step process . . . from acceptance to approval to adulation. And most of us never progress beyond awareness of this third stage of needs . . . probably because our perception of "need" keeps changing to more, more, and more . . . and is never satisfied.

If we do, however, feel a higher need, the next level is self-esteem: the feeling that "I can live with and respect myself, regardless of what others think of me." This is a high level. In my view, it comes very close to what God expects of us. To be transparent; to be without a need to perform for the judgment of others; to seek to do our best with no need to compete, no need to keep score—to do what we must because we must.

At the top—with all other needs satisfied—is the need to grow. Wow. This need has nothing to do with either esteem-by-others or self-esteem. No reward is sought. It's a hunger for growth for the sake of growth. You're so wrapped up in growing that it doesn't occur to you that it could be measured.

That seems a lot like love. If you really love, you never stop to measure how much, because there's no way to measure anyway. There's no goal, no competition, no fulfillment that ends the need. Perhaps it's like heaven—where I can't imagine the first four needs, but where I hope there is still the need for growth.

And so (at least it seems to me) that our reverence for #2 and #3 in this hierarchy of needs can lead to making them gods. And for the first four, our business and our job and our corporation can indeed be the prime candidates for fulfilling those needs. A good job can provide the biological needs, the security needs, the social needs, even the self-esteem needs—for the Leo in us, anyway. Growth need? Well, I think no single occupation can provide for it entirely. If a person's life is dominated by his role as businessman—even clergyman or social worker—it's hard to see how his need for growth (as a complete Christian) can be so limited in scope.

And so, for most of us, the corporate arena—whether that be a big company, a store, a trade union, a medical or law practice—is the great provider of opportunity to fulfill our most basic needs. And I hope we therefore respect them for that; there is nothing wrong with *them*. It's what we do with the opportunity.

For most of us, it's a ladder to climb from the bottom. But even for the inherited-wealth person (who may own the whole ladder because his entrepreneur grandfather willed it to him) it's his means to supply his need. He knows he will never want for food, shelter, or security, or even for the kind of social acceptance he can find at the country club. But he has a desperate need to prove his worth—his non-inherited worth—to others and, hopefully, to himself. And "doing a good job" is the most obvious way to prove himself. I hope we respect that, too.

For a lot of us, the Corporate Arena provides a nifty security blanket. With pride, a lot of people proclaim their 35 years of service to the corporation. That has always disturbed me. Am I being unfair to wish that, instead, we would talk about our 35 years of service to customers? Nor is it even service to *somebody* in the corporation; it's to the "thing" itself. Can longevity ("staying with the company until you are 65") become a god, too? I think it can. And if you want to serve that god, a big company can provide just what you're looking for—if you keep your nose clean, don't display religious pictures on your office wall or make waves about standard operating procedure.

Now that sounds snide. What's so awful about longevity and security?

I'm sorry. I don't mean they are wrong in themselves. I mean they *could,* if we seek them too fiercely, become gods for which we will offer sacrifice. It's the *seeking* that is the dangerous part.

Certainly you can rise to the top of an organization, earn a big salary, stay with the company for years, *have* security—without having them as goals. I know a lot of successful (highly paid) people who have been intent only on doing everything well—the very best they can. They are dedicated to excellence. But not a "my-company-right-or-wrong" sort of

39

loyalty. The money, promotions, and power came to them as a natural residual or by-product, not as something overtly sought. Their goals were talent-oriented or service-oriented, not profit- or power-oriented.

That's why I question the morality of a company setting its bottom-line profit goals first—and then making everything else make that happen. Bottom-line goals can cause sacrifice to and compromise of everything else. In fact, it's dangerous for a Christian to set even heaven as his bottom-line goal. He ought to seek loving and serving God and shining the Light before others. Heaven, too (I think) could become a god—more highly prized than God Himself.

What makes all this difficult is that so many of us condone and even admire the corporation that makes higher and higher profits, the man who reaches the top of the Corporate Ladder, the union that forces a higher and higher wage scale. Today, we are constantly reminded that it's "looking out for good ol' Number One" that counts.

Of course, you are expected to do all this legally. And ethically.

But no one regards "looking out for Number One" as illegal or unethical. Only Christianity has a law against that. It is neither illegal nor unethical to sacrifice everything for your corporation or your job or your security . . . or even to *proclaim* that they are your gods.

Enough! What is your conclusion? What is the point of all this?

Just this: A Leo-Christian ought to be at least aware that his business pursuits needn't be, but could be, honest-to-God gods. If he finds himself sacrificing his Christian principles to commercial principles or principals—his company's or his own—he has a real

41

Leo-Christian problem. Money, status, and security are the 20th-century idols—not graven calves or eagles.

And the decision involves sacrifice to the One God or to another god. If you let your Christian get in the way of your Leo, it can cost you money, a promotion, and even your job. But the alternative is costly in another way.

Okay, so you've made your point that business can become our god. Now will you STOP this examination of conscience?

I hope not. It's something I have to do daily.

4

Keeping The Sabbath Day Holy
vs
Keeping It Profitable

About half of the Ten Commandments still make pretty good sense to most Christians and Jews—at least in theory. You can't quarrel much with keeping God Number One, with honoring dad and mom; and murder, lying, and stealing have stayed clearly on the no-no list.

But some of the others have been modernized. When we hear of extramarital or premarital sex, it might elicit a tut-tut or a shrug of the shoulders—but a grin is more likely than outrage or shock or a prayer to God to forgive the person who sinned. (Or is sin obsolete, too?)

Coveting? Ha! That went out with button shoes— or at least with the Edsel. Maybe even with frankincense and myrrh. "Not coveting" is tantamount to "no ambition," isn't it?

Well, you've got to admit that coveting doesn't HURT anybody . . . as long as you don't actually DO anything.

We'll talk about that later. But for now, let's consider the Commandment about Keeping Holy the Sabbath Day . . . Sunday, for Christians.

This Commandment didn't go out with button shoes or even with the Edsel. But it's certainly on its way out now ... with the burgeoning success of super stores in shopping centers.

Of course, "keeping holy" is a matter of interpretation. Once Jesus was accused of blasphemy for curing somebody on the Sabbath.

The commandment still means "go to church if you can." But then, it can include (according to individual interpretation) puttering in the garden, playing golf with friends, playing with the children, painting the bathroom, watching pro football on TV, or catching up with the work you brought home from the office. But none of those is *directly* opposed to the preservation of Sunday as a non-commercial and therefore special day of rest from the pursuit of the almighty dollar.

But the new thrust is to make Sunday just another day of commerce. It's already a reality in many places. The yes vote—to repeal the blue laws—is overwhelming.

Now wait a minute! After all, many wives work all week and some husbands work on Saturday ... and being open on Sunday can be a form of "helping your neighbors" by giving them the opportunity to shop on Sunday. Besides, we can provide employment to people who would otherwise be on welfare. Think of the good in this!

Well, if that *is* the motivation, you make it sound pretty "holy."

But if I owned the store and decided to open it on Sunday, I would have to ask myself some questions.

"Am I really doing this to help people ... or to increase sales and profits?"

"Am I keeping people—employees and customers—away from church and away from family

45

togetherness? From experiencing God in their backyards or the zoo or just in having time to contemplate?

"Am I contributing to the idolization of commerce as a god and therefore to the decline of God in man's life?"

"Do I *need* the money?"

"Are my priorities out of order?"

"Will it further contribute to driving the small store owner out of business? Or at least drive him, too, to forsake the Sabbath and stay open to stay in business?"

And if I am a Sunday employee, I must ask myself:

"Do I *need* the money? Or am I working to be able to afford luxuries?"

"Did I skip church (because I *had* to go to work)?"

"Did I lose the opportunity to keep Sunday somehow holy as God said I should?"

And if I am a Sunday shopper, I must ask myself:

"Do I need this shopping on Sunday bit?"

"Am I causing these people to have to work today?"

"Am I contributing to the demise of the Lord's Day . . . and therefore to the demise of the worship of God?"

Somebody asked: "What if they gave a war and nobody came?" I ask: "What if they made Sunday a shopping day and nobody showed up—to work or to shop?"

So you can't blame only the entrepreneurs, the owners, the stockholders. We're all to blame.

Worse—if Sunday goes the way of all workdays—it may rob us Leo-Christians of our last justification for behaving less Christian in business than we do on Sunday. 'Till now, we could "make up for it" on the Sabbath.

Very funny!

That's really not a joke. For a Leo-Christian, the traditional Sunday—however "holy"—was at least non-Leo. It was a once-a-week opportunity to allow His Christian to run free of his Leo . . . 24 hours of "no conflict" with his personal or corporate goals.

Well, it may surprise you to hear this. But even I have my doubts about business-as-usual on Sunday.

Hmmm. That gives me an idea! What if it weren't "business as usual"? On Sunday, the employer would hire only the unemployed; he could sell at regular prices to those who could afford it but at cost (or free) to the poor . . . so that he could "break even" but make no profit on his Sunday business. That would be a nifty way to keep the Sabbath Day holy.

You are ridiculous. That is foolish and impossible.

Not impossible but foolish certainly. And didn't Paul say we should be fools for Christ? I know lots of people in social work and missionary work who are fools like that seven days a week.

And maybe there are still a few in business. In the good old days—and maybe even today in small towns—a village shopkeeper or artisan could be that kind of "holy fool" in business. Not only did he sell his goods or services to the poorer townsfolk at lower prices, he looked upon his business as a routine way to serve his neighbors. Of course, he had the advantage of *knowing* his customer/neighbors, not only by name but also as persons.

He could repair Tom Murphy's shoes or make him a coat or sell his wife a leg o' lamb or grind her a pound of coffee with some personal concern.

47

Well, that may be Christian; it's not what I'd call "holy."

Well, I would. I hope "holy" doesn't just refer to stuff you do on your knees with a candle in one hand and a Bible in the other. I think it's praising and serving God; and most of our opportunity as Leo-Christians is to do that through our neighbors ...during business hours.

Neighbors? Man, you can't even SEE neighbors in anything but the smallest kind of business today. In medium or big business, it's not only hard to recognize your neighbors ... it's difficult to even recognize them as people. Their names have become numbers, so at least the computer can recognize them. The manufacturer is not even in touch with the ultimate consumer; there's a whole network of shipper, distributor, wholesaler, and retailer in between. And even the "retailer" is a national chain (headquartered in Cincinnati or somewhere). For most of us, even the customer is not a person, but a corporation (headquartered in Schenectady or somewhere).

But . . .

But nothing! You simply can't survive in business if you try to be "holy" . . . whether it's Sunday or Tuesday. I'm not saying you have to be an antichrist. But you have to realize that Christianity is just not realistic or practical. Business is not "serving the public." It's "making a profit." It's a matter of cost + markup = selling price. It has very little to do with people.

Your definition of business reduces the purpose of work to "making money."

I guess that's why we have people in the dog food business who hate dogs, people in the furniture business who have no love for wood, people in the government business who have no interest in the governed.

We're in "marketing" (it doesn't matter what) or "manufacturing" (it doesn't matter what) or "investment" (it doesn't matter what) or "construction" (it doesn't matter what).

My dad used to say, "Choose your occupation first of all because you love doing it, because you enjoy it enough that you'd do it for no pay, because it fulfills you. If you love it you will be good at it, people will be served, and you will be happy. And you will also be paid enough money to sustain you. If you choose backwards (choose your occupation according to what it will pay you), you will be spending eight hours a day *working* in the worst sense of the word; you will hate it; you will not be fulfilled; you will never be satisfied with your pay because it will never be enough.

What? Your father was a plumber! That certainly wasn't what he CHOSE to do! How can you love fixing toilets?

My dad didn't just fix toilets, he fixed people's problems. He loved plumbing. He felt useful to people. He didn't fix leaky faucets; he fixed *people's* leaky faucets and stopped a needless waste of water. He was an environmentalist before the word was invented.

I remember the time I found out—thought I found out—that he misunderstood the whole principle of bidding on a job. For instance, Pop would bid $100 and get the job. When finished, if everything went better than expected and he figured he should have estimated $70, he'd charge the customer $70. But if it took longer than expected and should have been bid at $130, he would charge $100—just as he estimated. I told him he was crazy . . . that he should charge $100 in both cases OR charge $70 in the first instance and $130 in the second.

Obviously I am RIGHT. And my father was a stupid businessman. After all, he was only an immigrant with a fourth-grade education who started his own plumbing business when he was about 22 years old and still spoke broken English.

Pop grinned at me and said: "I'm not so dumb as you think. First of all, I don't average my customers. I serve one at a time. I can't pass my mistake in one case on to the next. Yet don't feel sorry for me. It

50

works out. In case you don't know it, it costs a lot of time and money to make estimates . . . to be competitive. I happen to have third-generation customers who never ask me for an estimate, never ask me to bid in competition with another plumber. They just call me and ask me to do the job. They trust me. It's a good feeling for both of us. But it's also profitable. It saves me money and saves them money. And it lets me concentrate on fixing their plumbing problem."

Your father had a point. But I bet he could have made a lot more money the other way.

Yes, I bet he could have.

And anyway, what's that got to do with holiness?

A lot, I think.

Would your father have worked on Sunday?

Sure . . . if somebody needed his help and it couldn't wait until Monday. But not to make an extra buck. There's a difference.

That's understandable in small business. But it's different in big business.

Does that mean a Leo-Christian doesn't have to be a Christian in big business—only in small business?

No. I didn't say that. I just said it's more difficult. After all, you can't restrict your employees or stockholders to just "Christians." It's against the law. And you can't foist Christian principles on everybody. That's not Christian.

You're right. It is difficult.

But you shouldn't think that God is completely ignored in business. I've been to a lot of business meetings in public—banquets, especially—when there *was* an *invocation. And I've heard chief operating officers . . . in their annual message to employees . . . say, "May God bless you."*

So have I. This may sound cynical—but I hope it's sincere. In America, it's still good public relations for a businessman to be seen going to church, and to recognize the Almighty in public. I'm not knocking it; I'm for it, if it's sincere. But I think the hard part is recognizing God in business when it's just between you and Him.

Don't be so harsh. After all, business in America doesn't completely deny religion. We still close on Christmas. Companies even send gifts to good customers in the spirit of the season.

Oh, that's right. They send a case of Chivas Regal to its best customer, half a case to its "B" customers, and a bottle of California wine to its "C" list. Of course, it has to adjust the figures somewhat because the IRS has limits.

For your information, I know a lot of companies who have stopped that.

Good. I only hope they stopped because it was demeaning to Christmas, not just because they feared being accused of payola.

You certainly are nasty about American business.

No, I'm not! I just don't happen to agree that American business *has to be* the way some American business has *become.*

You certainly can't deny that America is the prime example of business success and progress . . . with the world's highest standard of

living . . . and *it wouldn't have happened if it had remained a land of small, holy shopkeepers. As Calvin Coolidge said, "The business of America is business."*

I'm sure you're right. But I wish . . .

Well, stop wishing and face reality. Times have changed. You can't take your religion to work—not outwardly, anyway. You can't tack a crucifix to your office wall or display a religious picture on your desk. People would think you were weird. And besides, it would be a violation of the separation of church and state, of . . .

Yeah, I guess it would. You can't be an overt apostle . . . *at work* . . . can you?

No. There's Sunday for that.

For awhile, maybe. But . . .

Look. You mustn't take these things so seriously. After all, you can't stop the wheels of progress.

No, I suppose we'd be fools to try.

5

Love Each Other
As I Have Loved You
vs
The Law of Supply and Demand

Keeping the Ten Commandments (literally, anyway) is no sweat compared to the one John tells us that Jesus gave us: "Love one another as I have loved you."

I hope He was joking.

Even if He would settle for, "Do unto others as you'd want them to do unto you," I'll bet He's something less than overjoyed by how we're "doing unto each other" in the business world.

Like what?

Like lawsuits, for one: Sue your competitor. Sue the manufacturer. Sue anybody you can find in a loophole. And not just for damages, but for all you can get. (The insurance company will pay; and insurance companies aren't people!

Like Labor vs Management, for another: Strikes, Shutdowns, Lockouts, Violence, Bribes . . . and Ugly Animosity . . . anything to get everything-we-can-get for "our side."

Like prejudice. Strange, isn't it, that we had to *enforce* Equal Employment Opportunity in the land that supposedly is founded on equality as its most basic tenet? And let's not kid ourselves. So far, EEO isn't a principle we *believe;* it's a law we *comply* with (as minimally as possible) to stay out of court.

But you must be realistic. If you hire blacks or women or Indians in certain jobs, your customers or clients (if they're as prejudiced as most of us) will quit doing business with you! So, you'll be out of business and unable to hire ANYBODY . . . even white heterosexual males! And you'd put all of your current employees on the street! That's basic.

You could be right. But your argument is not as basic as the basic I'm talking about.

Well, you've got to admit the situation has improved.

Yes. I can remember when a U. of Michigan alumnus might reject an applicant because he went to Michigan State. Or turn somebody down because he was a Catholic or a Jew or a Protestant. Or had a beard. *That* doesn't happen anymore, of course!

You are being sarcastic, aren't you?

Who, me?

Well, let me ask you . . . and be honest: would YOU like it if YOU were the client of (say) a law firm you'd been dealing with for 10 years and suddenly they sent over a black woman lawyer to represent you—wouldn't that give you pause?

I would hope not. But, to be frank, I suspect it would.

See there!

See there, what? I'm still given pause at the idea of a lower-class Jewish carpenter being my Savior and King. I would feel better if He had had more "class." That's what I mean by basic.

I wish you would stop bringing religious con-siderations into business discussions. Christianity is just not practical or realistic. And business, to survive, must be both practical and realistic.

Yes, the Leo-Christian dilemma.

There you go again! Why can't you let Leo go to work and leave the Christian at home? It would be a lot simpler.

It sure would. Then I could without concern:
- ... fire a man with a family of six because I could hire a better replacement at the same salary,
- ... cut my price to break even, to take my competitor's customer away—because I can afford it and he can't.
- ... accept and promote "business" as neces-sarily a dog-eat-dog war:
  company vs company,
  labor vs management,
  buyer vs seller,

  even ME vs MY BEST FRIEND IN A RACE TO THE TOP OF THE CORPORATE LADDER.

- ... pay somebody less than he's worth because he's at my mercy and the savings will increase the corporate profit.
- ... maintain Rank-Has-Its-Privileges, executive perqs, and impressive titles to clearly sepa-rate hierarchy from ordinary employees. Address these employees by their first names but never tolerate the vice-versa; treat them as cogs in a well-oiled machine and never bother to wonder who they are as

"people" aside from being workers. Keep them frightened, aware that you are in a position to get them fired. But praise them and pat them on occasion, just as the circus performer throws a fish to the trained seals.

That's ridiculous! Who does that?

I do, for one. A lot of times I refer to "my secretary" (I know some guys who . . . worse . . . say "my girl") when I could simply say Mary Smith. To be honest, I cringe when she refers to me as "my boss." I don't like it because I wonder if that's because I *act* like a boss.

That is nitpicking.

Maybe. But these little things that exist in business make it hard to remember that our fellow-workers are fellow-human beings and fellow-Christians—that we are brothers and sisters in Christ. And it's even harder when we think of our customers as "target audiences" or "shares of market" or ***Neilsen Ratings*** . . . instead of people we love and want to serve with good products at a reasonable price. And it's almost impossible to extend "Love Thy Neighbor" to people in the same business we're in whom we routinely refer to as "the competition" or "the enemy."

If you're not careful, you'll destroy the whole idea of free enterprise in the name of Christianity. A Leo isn't really "out to get" those individual people as people. You can't think of them as people or fellow-Christians. If somebody's in the way of progress—or a sale—you regard him merely as an obstacle to be overcome, a hurdle to be jumped, a pawn to be moved

in the fascinating game of commerce. It's not personal.

I agree. It's *not* personal. And I suspect that the less "personal" business gets, the easier it becomes to excuse ourselves from loving one another as Jesus loved us. We can come to feel unconfronted by that law . . . and observe instead the Law of Supply and Demand.

What? Now what's wrong with the Law of Supply and Demand? It's the whole basis of our free enterprise system, isn't it? I've always thought of it as being part of the Constitution and the Bill of Rights. How could you be negative about the Law of Supply and Demand?

Well, frankly, I don't know whose law it is. It certainly ain't mentioned in or even implied in either the Constitution *or* the Bill of Rights. In fact, I suspect it isn't because—when you think about it—the law of supply and demand is as undemocratic as it is unchristian. And, if taken literally, it's anti-free enterprise.

Whaa . . . aa . . . t??!!?

It's a law that makes it OK for the Haves to put the Have-nots at their mercy. It sanctifies cornering the market on anything and making everybody else pay your price. If a Big Corporation bought all the water (and it's not too far-fetched an idea at that) it could price it at $3 a quart if it wanted to, because it would have all the supply and everybody else would have the demand.

The government wouldn't allow such a monopoly.

Which proves my point. The law of supply and

61

demand is *not* "democratic" and **is** "anti-free enter-prise." **It is theoretically abusive.**

Well, carried to the extreme, I guess you're right. But we don't permit monopoly.

How much less wrong is a Tri-opoly or Quadr-opoly—having the supply in the hands of *three* or *four* big corporations?

If they're in cahoots together, it could be pretty terrible. But competition . . . which is what I mean by free enterprise . . . will keep the situation under control and even "good" for the people.

I hope so. And I'm for that 100 percent; but I worry about "Saturday Night Specials" (big corporations buying out others in forced mergers). "Making an offer they can't refuse" used to be regarded as Mafia tactics, but now it's standard business practice. If your "supply" of money is big enough, you can "demand" that somebody sell you his business even if he doesn't want to. That's "enterprise" all right, but it's not my idea of "free." And if it goes unbridled, pretty soon we'll have two or three huge corporations that own us all.

What's this got to do with "love thy neighbor" . . . which I thought was the subject of this discussion?

Everything, I think. When the **people** in a company can feel that the purpose of their labor is customer satisfaction . . . providing worthwhile products or services for the price . . . it's very possible to be in business for the **purpose** of "loving" (being of service to) others. Business is beautiful when the seller is glad that the customer is pleased with the product's worth and the buyer is glad to pay the seller his price, including a fair profit.

A company (a group of people working together in community to produce good products or services at a fair price) is beautiful. If it is a large shoe company, proud of its craftmanship and marketing skill (not unlike the individual shoemaker in the olden days), Halleluiah! Glory be to God!

But what if the company becomes obsessed with ownership, profits, growth as a *priori* goals—without regard to its *business* (what it provides for its customers)? What if it regards the cunning of its legal and financial officers far more highly than the artisanship or professionalism, creativity or sweat of its workers . . . as, in fact, the *core* of its "business"? What if it can use its money power to buy a company that doesn't want to be bought, or force a competitor out of business, or corner the supply of a commodity so that it can practically dictate an exorbitant price? And what if it can do these things without pangs of conscience?

I merely submit that it's gonna get harder for a Leo-Christian to love his neighbor unless we stop this perverted, impersonal, **passionate, paranoid, pagan,** and **parasitic preoccupation** with **profit** for **power to purchase the world.** It can end with the ultimate shoot-out . . . in Wall Street. Not between nations nor races nor ideologies nor religions (for all those who will have been purchased). Maybe IBM's computers vs Mitsubishi's . . . winner takes all.

> And then somebody's "Hal" will own us all.
> The loser will fall and spill its green
> blood all over the floor of the New York
> Stock Exchange, emitting
> a dying oath of allegiance to the
> dollar or yen.

It would be just my luck to have stock in the wrong company.

6

Thou Shalt Not Kill
vs
The Competitive Spirit

Any Leo-Christian worth his Gucci shoes, vice-presidency, company-issued philodendron plant . . . or any other business equivalents of the athlete's uniform . . . *must* have a fierce competitive spirit. Right?

Now don't tell me you question the virtue of a competitive spirit!

I question a lot of things lately.

Next you'll be telling me you're an advocate of "New Games" . . . like the Girl Scouts.

The truth is I've tried. I've told myself that New Games are right and beautiful and a spiritual experience, etc. But I still like choosing sides, keeping score, and going at it!

Especially in business. The Corporate Arena is no place for laughing children running hand-in-hand through a meadow of wildflowers toward the welcoming arms of Jesus.

Oh, it's not just business. I love my brother-in-law; but when we play golf, it's "heavenly" to go into the 18th tied and experience a 30-foot blast from a sandtrap fly into the holy for a birdie . . . to crush his anticipation of victory as he taps in his craftsmanlike but inadequate par.

I admit to the thrill of being promoted (above others) by my company. I thoroughly enjoy having my proposal accepted in a meeting over the counter-proposals of others. And (no doubt!) it's more fun to beat out a competitor in a head-to-head *battle* for a new account than to be *awarded it automatically,* without competition, merely because our company has a good reputation and track record.

So what's wrong with the competitive spirit?

I used to think: nothing. But when I see what it breeds, I'm not so sure.

It breeds love of war. Of war, per se. Us against Them; Me *vs* Somebody; Victor vs Vanquished. We can pretend it's just a friendly 50¢ Nassau with who-cares-who-wins-and-nobody-gets-hurt; but let's be honest. The Competitor . . . the kind we admire in business or sport . . . is a General-Patton-with-a-briefcase, a Jack-the-Ripper-sliding-into-second-with-his-spikes-aimed-at-the-shortstop's-jugular. If there's no enemy, there's no fun; if there's no blood, there's no champagne; we savor new customers like fresh scalps; if everybody in the company is a vice-president, it's no prize to become a vice-president; when somebody gets promoted, everybody else feels demoted.

That's right. But what's wrong with that?

When it gets to be an obsession, we will do anything to win. Even kill.

Kill? Kill whom?

Anybody who is in the way.

You're talking about the Mafia. Sure, they'll kill to protect their business. (I know because I saw the movie). And maybe there have been a few union-vs-union killings. But you're talking about gangster stuff, not normal business. Corporations don't have guns.

Not guns. But weapons, surely. Money. Power. Threats. You can strangle, shoot down, choke, stab, kill off a competitor ... be it an individual or a company ... with a ball-point pen, a sharp tongue, a pointed paragraph in a letter, a look, a snicker, a half truth, a comment ... or no comment.

Kill? Oh, that kind of kill! I thought you meant literal killing.

I do and I don't. Both.

The obsession *can* cause literal killing. Maybe not murder, but manslaughter.

Cost-cutting, efficiency, beating-the-competition to the marketplace, "taking advantage of opportunity when it knocks" have killed mineworkers, chemical workers, factory workers, farmworkers. They have created products that have killed consumers ... with sugar, tar and nicotine, chemicals I can't pronounce, tires that blow, gas tanks that explode at a 5 mph impact, etc.

God only knows how many people of future generations will be killed by our environmental sins in the name of free enterprise and marketing goals.

But not on PURPOSE!

No. But *with* purpose: the purpose of Killing the Competition and/or Making a Killing. And so we limit our responsibility to "what we can get by with" (what is legally defensible) or "what can't be proved one way or the other for awhile."

Most environmental concerns are long range. You're talking about years, maybe decades!

Is killing *slowly* okay? Is paying starvation wages, or working an employee to death, less sinful than slashing his wrists and watching him bleed?

Well, it's more civilized.

And less criminal.

But hardly anybody in America pays starvation wages or works people to death anymore.

No. And just so I don't come off as a complete foe of unions, I think we can thank unions for removing our "opportunity" to get by with that. And minimum-wage laws, etc. But it's not 100 percent. I could show you some unskilled laborers, some migrant farmworkers, some . . .

Never mind.

Or perhaps we could go down and take a look at Skid Row. The alcoholics and drug addicts in this country are . . .

Now wait a minute! You're not blaming that on business, are you?

I'm not really blaming anything or anybody for anything. I'm just wondering—"taking inventory."

I know little about the *causes* of alcoholism or any other kind of chemical dependency . . . but "not being able to cope" is certainly one of them. Cope with what? With the need to compete? With the fear of failure? With realism as it exists in a "dog-eat-dog," "more-is-better," "win-or-lose," "kill the opposition" kind of real world?

Sure, alcoholics are sick. But are we all sick, too? Are we sick enough to "teach" young people with "executive potential" that martinis and scotch-on-the-rocks are an essential part of business life? That ordering a Coke or a glass of milk at a client lunch is unacceptable behavior? And when one of these proteges becomes an addict, do we shrug it off as an unusual case ("Too bad about young Charles; he had great potential but just couldn't hold his liquor") because we, too, are blind to the realities of alcoholism?

Aw, come on. There are a lot of alcoholics (and certainly most of the drug addicts) who have never been INSIDE the Corporate Arena.

True. But can they still feel the pressure? What about the excessive emphasis on winning in the Little League, in college and pro football, in the classroom . . . by well-intentioned businessmen/fathers/alumni who demand it of their kids and their alma mater just as they demand it of themselves?

You're suggesting "New Games" for the Big Ten, the NFL, or the Southwest Conference?

Perhaps Cosell would do the play-by-play.

Seriously, aren't you going too far in this introspection of business as a source of killing? After all, killing is pretty extreme.

Well, if you'd like to get less morbid . . . let's think about some of the killing we do as Leo-Christians that isn't mortal: We can kill someone's enthusiasm, self-esteem, joy, hope, incentive, reputation, etc. In so many offices and factories, everybody's so *serious* about reaching goals, protecting prerogatives, collecting kudos and other symbols of "success," that it truly seems like a commercial battlefield. War. (And all's fair in love and war, isn't it?)

We kill little parts of each other and each other's lives . . . with verbal knives-in-the-back, poisoned glances, threats-disguised-as-humor, cold shoulders, hierarchy of titles . . . in the elevator, halls, and john as well as in the board room or president's office.

Companies spend a lot of money to build employee morale. But is it really concern for employee enjoyment and happiness? Or is it purely morale for the sake of productivity? I think there's a major difference.

Well, productivity IS a problem these days. The unions do all they can to get more money for less work. And talk about killing? Unions have caused parity wages and parity output. A hard worker can't make a dime more than a goof-off. And if a person does work harder or faster, he's in trouble. Unions promote the feeling among workers that the employer is the enemy: Kill his time, kill his profits, and so-what-?-if-it-kills-his-business. And in the process, the union and the time-killing goof-off can kill the jobs of all of their fellow-workers.

Yes. And perhaps worse are some *other* fatalities of union extremism: a man's love of his individual craftsmanship . . . that marvelous feeling of doing more than he's paid to do, merely because he wants to . . . the genuine Christian need to like his boss, to feel goodness toward his company's bigshots, because he recognizes them as fellow sons of God.

You surely make "thou shalt not kill" cover a lot of miscellaneous territory.

Maybe. I know zilch about theology. I'm only interested in religion. To me, what's important is whether we think God will allow Leo-Christians to

71

write off these sins as "legitimate business expenses" merely because they were committed on company time.

As bigshots or middle managers or foremen or nobodies . . . in a company or union . . . we're all part of a production line which can "produce" good or evil to each other as well as good or bad products.

As competitors or fellow-workers or suppliers or customers, we have the potential to kill—as groups or as individuals.

But do you really think it's worse now than it ever was? Is today's Corporate Arena . . . big business . . . more dangerous?

In my opinion, yes. The elephants are fighting. And getting bigger. The monkeys have all climbed the trees or have sold out to the elephants.

Many businessmen I know are convinced that our real wars (the ones supposedly between nations or ideologies) are just "fronts" for corporate wars. Patriots and zealots are dying on real battlefields, killed by real guns and spilling real blood; but they are unknowing warriors for the cause of some commercial elephant's financial interests, raw materials, or land or mineral rights.

True?

I have no idea. What I do know is that right here in America, in every office building and factory and supermarket, there are millions of us who use weapons to do really destructive things to others. The weapons are telephones and typewriters and business forms and other tools of our trade. It's caused . . . I think . . . by super-extreme emphasis on "success" and the competitive spirit. By a drive to drive everybody else out of business, to kick others off the ladder of success so that we can climb it.

I have made brutal remarks about a client, a fellow-worker, a competitor—sometimes merely because we have not seen eye to eye. I have often destroyed or damaged someone's self-confidence, crushed his spirit, or bruised his pride. I honestly think I have never done it intentionally ("murderously"); but my standard excuse—"not being tolerant of mediocrity"—does not absolve me of what I consider a kind of "manslaughter."

But—and I don't say this to boast but to show that it can be done—I have also interjected questions, objections, humor, or alternative suggestions into business discussions that seemed to be coming perilously close to the brink of "bad." I am certain that more "minor Watergates" or "decisions that wouldn't make the saints applaud" could be avoided if someone in the meeting or company would even **raise an eyebrow**.

Of course, if you get a reputation for doing that, you might not be invited into the next executive meeting.

Maybe you're right. But I have faith that **most** people **want** to do right . . . that they're glad when someone stops a company policy or decision that could wind up hurting or killing somebody.

And if you're wrong? What if the company dislikes your Christian input to Leo considerations?

You get fired. Or demoted. Or ignored. But that's the test of your Leo-Christian commitment. It's easy to say but hard to do. I have not really had many tests; I sometimes wish I had, just to see if I had the guts and stuff to let my Christian wrestle with my Leo in a serious confrontation.

I have wondered: If I were a middle-manager (with no direct say-so) in an automobile company which was contemplating a cut in quality to save a few cents on a part . . . would I speak up to my superiors and say, "I don't think we should do this"? Or would I just close my eyes and pray that nobody would be killed if the part broke?

I hope you aren't accusing . . .

I am saying only this: We have become so obsessed with winning that the purpose of business has become a sort of war. It isn't "providing goods and services"; it isn't "providing jobs for people"; it isn't "making a livelihood" . . .

It is war. And we will kill to conquer, to acquire, to dominate.

If there were less stress on profits, market share, whipping the opposition, acquisition, getting to be Number One, climbing the corporate ladder . . . and more stress on pride in our product, love of our craft, serving our customers, the welfare of our employees . . .

You are dreaming. You are a damned fool.

A fool maybe—but not damned.

7

Thou Shalt Not Adulterate
vs
Cheating on Written and
Unwritten Contracts

To begin with, you've adulterated the wording and the meaning of the commandment. "Adultery" and "adulterate" are not the same thing.

Not exactly. But they're both forms of cheating on a promise and a contract . . . being unfaithful to someone you have explicitly or implicitly promised faithfulness.

Why don't you stick with adultery? There is certainly some of that in the Corporate Arena . . . businessmen cheating on their wives, businessmen procuring prostitutes for customers, women-in-business getting promotions and salary increases for "favors granted."

So I've heard. But I really don't rank those among the tough Leo-Christian dilemmas. They may happen often enough . . . honestly, I don't know. Perhaps I've been in sheltered groups, but I've never been "propositioned" . . . nobody has ever offered to "fix me up" . . . and I haven't ever been asked to provide those kinds of customer favors. I have obviously seen plenty of signs of hanky-panky, but I seldom suspected it was business-related.

Don't you think, with the influx of women into higher corporate positions, that it's gonna get to BE a factor?

Well, it's certainly a weapon. Could be. But we've got enough to think about now without projecting. And anyway, the kind of Leo-Christian I have in mind would much rather play a round of golf with a client or make a sale than play hanky-panky.

If he does have a sex problem . . . this Leo-Christian . . . it's more likely to be in the area of "using" sex, sensuality, prurient interests . . . to sell whatever it is he's selling. If you own or work in a store that sells books, is it okay to sell what you consider dirty books? If you run a movie theatre, a motel, or an apartment building . . . you might have a decision. But all kinds of products . . . which are pure on the surface . . . can be sold, packaged, and advertised in ways that ought to cause a conflict in the Leo-Christian's guts. Is it okay to advertise in *Hustler* or *Club*—even if it really sells the stereos you're selling? Is it okay to name or promote a perfume or pantyhose or sports cars or jewelry or bedsheets as if you're also promoting adultery? And the tough part is . . . if you aren't calling the shots, if it wasn't your idea, but you're a link in the chain and expected to carry out company policy . . . what do you do then? You can (a) keep quiet and do it; or (b) let the company know you don't approve of it and are doing it reluctantly; or (c) raise a stink, refuse to participate, and risk getting fired; or (d) quit and go somewhere else.

What would you do?

Being essentially chicken, I have most often

settled for (b). A few times I have braved (c). I have never done either (a) or (d).

Of course, I must admit that I haven't been challenged all that much. And I doubt that most people have or will. Most people in the driver's seat will back off or adjust, if challenged, because they are essentially Leo-Christians, too. I myself have been the **proposer**, at times, of things I'm not exactly proud of—at least sophomoric-suggestive phrases or appeals.

But really, don't you think business . . . even the advertising part of business . . . is pretty tame, adultery-wise or sex-wise, compared to the real world?

I agree. If the real world lived as "happily married" and as "faithful" and as "family-oriented" and as puritanical as the people in McDonald's or Betty Crocker or Budweiser or Milky Way commercials . . . we'd be in great shape.

But you don't think the business world comes off so well in the area of adulteration?

Right.

Like what, specifically?

Like phony "cents off" labels. Like getting a contract by making a low bid . . . and then substituting inferior materials without telling anybody. Like putting certain products in your store "on sale" and then surreptitiously upping the prices on other items to even it out. Like reducing the quality of ingredients in a product that has been on the market for a long time . . . without reducing the price or telling the customer it ain't the same product. Like promising one thing and doing another. Like charging for services you didn't do.

80

Like inventing a special tool to fix something in a car that will need replacement . . . merely to make the consumer bring it to the dealer to get it fixed.

Like collusion between two bidders. Like payola. Like kickbacks. Like bribes. Like favors and lavish entertainment for customers.

What? That's not adulteration.

I think it is. It's cheating. For one thing . . . if you report it as a "legitimate cost of doing business" for tax purposes . . . it's either cheating or not deductible. If it isn't cheating the government, it could be cheating your competitors, who may not be able to match your money or your (low) moral standards. Or cheating your own company's stockholders or employees.

Adulteration, to me, is unfaithfulness . . . not delivering the goods or services you promised or led somebody to expect, not being faithful to fair free enterprise.

An employee is guilty of it when he cheats on his employer . . . by goofing off or doing sloppy work or faking illness. Buyers do it by playing one supplier against another . . . or by misusing power to get a bargain; worst of all, by *giving* business according to "favors granted."

Companies and individuals do it by "going bankrupt" to avoid taxes; and banks do it by advising those people to *do* it.

But adultery . . . adulteration? Isn't that a curious way to think about cheating? It isn't even sexual.

I doubt that God had only sexuality in mind when he made the Law against adultery. I think it was a Law against unfaithfulness, a law that said you ought to live up to your promises and your responsibilities.

But . . . if it will make you feel any better . . . I

81

could say that all this is prostitution: "Doing it" for money.

Now THAT sounds more like adultery. I'm pleased. Can you give me another example?

Well, one of the standard arguments concerns American corporations that are dealing with foreign countries or companies who expect to be paid bribes or kickbacks . . . even though it's against American laws, or American ideals.

Yes, what about that? If it's the only way to compete . . . and if it isn't illegal for them . . . why is it wrong for an American corporation to do what's necessary?

What's the question?

I take it you mean the choice is obvious.

For a Leo-Christian, I think it is.

You are being idealistic.

I hope so.

Thou Shalt Not Steal
vs
Knowing a Perq
When You See One

I have the feeling that this could be the hairiest of all.

So do I. We must have a guilty conscience.

But you don't really steal. Nice people don't steal. Lie, maybe. Or commit adultery or cuss or be mean to their neighbor or competitor. But steal?

When I was growing up, I remember vividly thinking how awful, how unthinkable it was to steal. I certainly thought that stealing was done only by the deprived or the depraved—never by white-collar society.

Ah, yes. But we have people in the highest places embezzling, laundering money, doing funny-business with bank loans . . .

Hey, I thought we were not going to discuss crime, per se.

But some of these people really thought it was okay to . . . well . . . "borrow money" from "their own" bank without paying interest, have "their own" government employees do major repairs on their home, etc.

You may be right. It certainly sounds like they thought it was okay. But let's start with us . . . with a lot of us . . . who think it's "okay" to . . .

What?

Well, like people who think it's okay to take home a supply of pencils, paper, ballpoint pens, paper clips, and rubber bands. Or to make personal long-distance phone calls and rig it so that the company pays for them. Or to use company stamps to mail personal letters and packages . . . even personal CHRISTMAS cards!

That is nitpicking!

Maybe. It also may be sophisticated white-collar petty larceny. I don't think our average white-collar office has ever calculated the cost of "take-home" items, but I'd bet it's staggering.

What is a company to do? Send out a memo saying "Don't Steal!" . . . frisk its employees before they leave for lunch and again at 5 o'clock? The employees would scream bloody murder!

Yes, they would . . . justified or not. I'm not proposing that companies do anything, really. I'm only proposing that I . . . as an individual . . . stop doing it if I do it. It's really not hard to know whether this is being taken home for "company work" or for "strictly home use." And I suspect that "pencils and paper clips" . . . in some cases are typewriters, calculators, reams of paper, boxes of envelopes, rolls of stamps, or quantities of the product the company manufactures or sells.

An American Management Association study

recently determined that "employee pilferage" adds up to *10 billion dollars a year* . . . which is FIVE TIMES as much as shoplifting. The only thing that matches it is commercial bribery—which is not usually regarded in the same sin league. White collar crime costs $40,000,000,000 a year . . . raises the retail price of goods 15 to 30 cents on a dollar . . .

I have a hunch you're still talking about petty larceny . . . on an individual basis. A lot of nickel-and-dime swipes that add up.

Well, if you're at the top of a company . . . if you're on a pretty liberal expense account . . . if you're the one who okays his *own* expense account or "has an understanding" with whoever does . . . you can do bigger things. Things that aren't even included in that AMA study because they're in a much higher class of "taking things."

You mean yachts, company cars not used much for company business, country clubs, travel to exotic places with wives . . . ?

I really mean less obvious things. Some executives in this country never buy a drop of whiskey; their "home" bars are supplied with company-bought liquor and they serve it to friends and neighbors who have no connection with business. I mean furniture . . . desks, TV sets, etc. I mean lunch. The secretaries and normal employees make a lot less money than the bigshots . . . and have to budget closely to buy a sandwich and a glass of milk at noon. Many of our country's highest-paid executives **rarely** buy their own lunch . . . a lunch of two martinis, steak, salad, coffee, and first-class service.

But those are business lunches! These people are WORKING during lunch! It's the cost of doing business.

I know that. I also happen to think there is something "almost Christian" about conducting business over a lunchtable . . . breaking bread together. People who do business together should be friends, should get to know each other . . . and having lunch together is a good way to do that. I think families would be stronger if they still had breakfast together and dinner together.

As Tevya in "Fiddler on the Roof" would say, "It's TRADITION!" And in business, too. That's why the government allows it as a legitimate tax deduction.

And I think they're right to do that.

So what's your complaint?

Well, I just wonder about the abuse. A customer who *expects* it . . . and lets that expectation be known . . . can be taken to lunch every day, *every single day.* Buyer and seller can arrange it . . . so that they both get free lunch everyday. You could get so used to it that, even if you have lunch alone, it somehow gets on the expense account.

Hey, that would be lying, not stealing. That belongs in ANOTHER CHAPTER!

If it's lying for the purpose of stealing, I think we might as well cover it here.

Well, expense accounts in general: There must be enough specific ways to steal on an expense account that it would take a book, not just part of a chapter.

And, I suspect, a lot of it is done by people who think they're "not really stealing" . . . just "doing what I have to do to make up for those exorbitant income taxes I have to pay in my tax bracket."

I'm not so sure they think about it much one way or the other.

What?

I mean, you just learn: As you climb the corporate ladder, you learn that there are special privileges. If you're an executive and can easily afford to buy your own coffee, you get free company-paid-for coffee . . . but if you're down the line, and you can't buy coffee without scrimping on something else, you have to buy your own coffee from the machine. It's an executive perq. It comes with advancement. It's not stealing.

I didn't say I thought it was stealing . . . necessarily. If it's all open and above board, fine. There are lots of ways to compensate an employee: salary, nicer offices, a country club membership, etc. Even more vacation. Most executives work lots of overtime, without extra pay . . . and therefore extra vacation seems perfectly justifiable.

Then perqs are okay?

If they're open and published, sure. Of course, they represent a problem for the Leo-Christian if he exults in his perqs . . . if he starts feeling superior (as a human being). If he starts **feeling** that "I'm first class" and everybody else is a peon. I'm not sure that perqs are good for Leo-Christians.

But it's not necessarily STEALING.

No. But the truth is that few perqs are publicized, common knowledge. Some aren't even "recorded." In certain positions, you can just "take" things. And it's not just the guys at the top. An awful lot of people in the middle . . . in charge of a supply room, a purchasing agent's secretary, a mailroom clerk, a financial department assistant . . . can "procure" or "okay" or "write off" something as a business expense that he or she *knows* is for personal, non-business use . . . either his own or some friend's. And taking something that rightfully belongs to the company (or to the government in the form of taxes) is stealing, isn't it?

But you really don't think, do you, that there's a lot of conscious stealing in business? I mean, most business people would NOT take money off your desk if you left it there unguarded . . . or rig the books . . . or dip into the petty cash drawer.

No, they wouldn't. And most shoplifters in a retail store would not take cash out of the register or pick the pocket of the proprietor. But they think taking merchandise is "not exactly stealing" like taking cash is stealing. Or a clerk, short-changing somebody dumb enough to "not notice."

Stealing someone else's ideas is even more polished. An individual who takes another's idea and presents it as his own . . . for the purpose of getting a raise in pay or even recognition . . . is stealing. Companies do it, too: They take another company's idea or product, copy it, and sell it.

But that's business, man! If somebody has an idea and you have the marketing skill, the money, and the machinery to cash in on his idea before he does, more power to you.

Isn't that a little like saying: If a man leaves a ten-dollar bill on a counter while he goes to the bathroom, and you have the opportunity to get to it before he gets back . . .

You are mixing business morality with personal morality.

91

I guess I am. When I was a kid I had an idea for a way to merchandise trade schools; I went to a few trade schools to tell them about my plan and some were very encouraging. Two weeks later I found that they had a meeting and decided to adopt my plan themselves, cutting me out. I couldn't sue; I had no money to sue; I was 17 years old and didn't even know what "sue" meant anyway.

They stole your idea.

I don't think they really thought it was stealing. It was simply taking advantage of an opportunity when it knocked. Why pay a 17-year-old kid for an idea when he wouldn't know what to do with it anyway?

In big business, that wouldn't have happened. There are laws.

I'm not discussing laws like that. I'm discussing laws of God. If you steal, and don't get caught . . . I have a hunch that Somebody up there has made a note of it.

If that happened to you today . . . those people stealing your idea . . . what would you do now that you didn't do then?

Maybe I would sue. But I hope not. I hope I would do what I did when I was 17: listen to the Holy Spirit, chalk it up to experience, and pray that the guys who stole my idea would really feel bad about it and ask God's forgiveness.

You DID that?

Yes. But you must realize: I was only 17 and very naive.

Thou Shalt Not Lie
vs
The Stupidity of Honesty in Business

I trust, during this discussion, that you are going to recognize that there's a huge difference between "bearing false witness" and fabricating an interesting reason for being late to a business meeting?

I hope so.

And I hope you realize that it's getting tougher to get away with "false and misleading" claims for a product . . . because the government is really cracking down.

Sure. But isn't that too bad? If we have to have the government monitor our truthfulness, it's gotten pretty sad.

What caused it was a really widespread use of lies . . . in advertising, on packages, in personal salesmanship. Products were advertised to cure colds when the manufacturer knew darn well they wouldn't; big boxes, half filled with product, appeared on the shelf to visually lie about the quantity of product inside; rigged comparisons, rigged research, weasel-worded guarantees-that-weren't-guarantees-of-anything were rampant.

Then you're for government control of this sort of thing?

Yes and no. I certainly wish that Free Enterprise were trustworthy enough to be Free to be Enterprising. But Ralph Nader and others have uncovered enough cases of Business Lying to the Public that I agree that something had to be done. But . . . like everything else these days . . . the judgments are strictly legal and letter-of-the-law. I can see that you shouldn't claim that these tennis shoes will make you run as fast as an Olympic champion; but you ought to be able to say that they'll help you jump "high enough to touch the tip of a star." I wish Business could earn back its right to be poetic and trusted.

And it isn't trusted?

No.

But is government trusted?

No.

What happened?

I truly think . . . bigness. Governments and corporations and stores have gotten so huge that there is no "person" to stand for truth. And if there is a "corporate lie" or a "government lie" it becomes impossible to pinpoint the source of that lie. It just "grew"; "somebody" passed it on to "somebody," who then passed it on to others . . . and it "became." Nobody approved of it.

How many people, every day, sign something they know is false! ("It came from upstairs" or "I'm just doing my job!") How many are parties to furnishing false information (verbal or printed) to a customer, to employees, to the government, to suppliers.

95

But are you talking about out-and-out lies or just "generally-accepted standards of truth in business"?

Both, I suspect.

But you can't expect business to be truthful in the same way you'd expect your family or friends to be truthful. You can't expect a job applicant to volunteer what's wrong with him . . . you can't expect a manufacturer to print on the package how much profit is in it for the manufacturer, or to tell you about a competitor's product that is virtually the same thing at a lower price.

Who said I did? I would no more expect that than I'd expect someone to tell his faults to his fiancee or his sins to his son . . . unless they asked.

Then what are you talking about?

I'm thinking about **half**-truths, distortions, overstatements, uncompleted comparisons, suppression of pertinent facts USED to get someone to believe something that **isn't** true.

I'm talking about making products appear to be something they aren't, through design or packaging or name or substitute materials.

And I am *not* talking about advocacy. As a salesman or an advertiser or a retail store, you may think a certain product is crummy; but if you think the manufacturer really believes it's great, you certainly can be its advocate. However, if you think the manufacturer is *lying* about the product (what it's made of or what it will do) . . . I happen to think you ought to deal yourself out of that business . . . that you're as guilty as he is.

If that's true, you probably think it's wrong to tell the boss or a customer you agree with him when you really don't.

It depends.

Oh, oh. You're hedging.

Not really. If the boss says he thinks that new secretary is attractive and you don't . . . I think it would be stupid to tell him you think she's ugly. But if he says he thinks such-and-such should be done as a business decision . . . and you tell him you agree when actually you disagree . . . I think that's a lie.

If a customer calls and asks about a delivery that's due and it's sitting on your desk and you tell the customer, "It's on the way over" . . . I think that's a lie.

If you interview a job applicant you have no intention of hiring or even considering and you say, "We'll give you a call, one way or the other, when we've made a decision" . . . and you don't . . . that's a lie.

If a pest calls and you don't want to talk to him, so you tell your secretary to tell him you're out of town . . . that, I think, is a lie.

If you goof up a job and you explain it to your customer by saying it was the fault of the supplier or the weather or something . . . I think that's a lie.

But you can't go around telling the truth about those things and expect to stay in business! People EXPECT you to lie a little.

Yes, and maybe that's why Business has such a lousy reputation. Maybe that's why we all have to hire so many lawyers to protect our loopholes. Maybe that's why we have so many regulatory agencies.

It's gotten so bad that you hardly know what to believe. If a company announces that John Brown resigned . . . you don't know whether he really resigned or got fired because the word "resign" is used in both cases.

But, being practical, you must admit that sometimes it's bad business to tell the truth . . . and even more often, the truth is inconvenient or inefficient.

I know. But I wonder if we haven't gotten in the habit of lying so often that we think nothing of it. I wonder, if we were a little more creative, couldn't we accomplish the purpose by saying something else? . . . something that isn't a lie? And I even wonder if we wouldn't get more respect and more business if . . . once in a while anyway . . . we didn't duck the truth. If we admitted that the late package was still sitting on the desk . . . that we just plain forgot to send it.

You're a dreamer. And impractical.

Not really. I know of many instances when it was done and it was so refreshing . . . if at first so shocking . . . that it was a big relief to everybody. Once we misjudged the scope of a job and we weren't ready to present a plan we had promised at a certain time. "What shall we tell the client?" somebody moaned. "Let's tell him the truth," somebody suggested. "What a fantastic idea!" everybody gasped. And so we did. And the client said, "Okay, I wouldn't want you to present something that wasn't ready; I want to be sure you really have thought through what you're recommending."

But what if he didn't react that way? What if he screamed and cussed and threatened to take his business elsewhere?

Well, you could always call back and tell him you lied about not being ready . . . that the truth is you were ready but the building caught fire and burned up the plans but you'll get going on new ones right away.

You sound like you've had practice.

I'm surely not contending that I've never lied . . . especially for convenience and sometimes to save face or save my skin. But always, in retrospect, I wished I hadn't; and I also realized that there was a better way to handle the situation.

I remember vividly a new young man we hired. He accidently stepped on some film and ruined it. Someone asked him, "What are you going to tell the boss?"

And what did he say?

He said, "Why, I'm going to tell him I stepped on the film."

And what happened?

Well, he established a reputation for honesty. And guts. Of course, he had a lot of other qualifications, too. But, in any event, he soon became head of the department.

10

Thou Shalt Not Covet
vs
Increasing Your Share
of Market

Of all the commandments, this one seems to differentiate most clearly between what is legal or ethical and what is moral (or Christian).

It certainly isn't against the law of the land to covet. Nor is it considered unethical. In fact, it's encouraged. The Leo-Christian who isn't intent on taking somebody else's share of market . . . who doesn't want to increase his share even if it's already 82.5 percent . . . is not worthy of his Leo.

Coveting is a sin. But it certainly isn't a sin, is it, to want to increase your share of market or to be ambitious . . . to aspire to your boss's job?

Well, I guess the "fine line" is determined by whether you're being greedy or not . . . by whether you feel jealousy or hate . . . by how you feel about it. It's the difference between "planning" your own actions and "plotting" to get somebody else's job, somebody else's business, somebody else's employees.

I guess I think that **none** of the other sins of business would happen if covetousness did not come first. You can want something very badly . . . for yourself or for your company . . . without feeling any greed or covetousness. If you just want to get better at what you're doing, want to please your customers more, want to be more valuable to your company. **But not at the expense of somebody else, not by taking away what somebody else already has.**

But what if you're not like that but your company is? And what if you're satisfied with your job and income but your WIFE nags you about getting a promotion, more money?

Well, that's their covetousness problem . . . or hers. If you want to, you can make it yours. Or not.

I happen to think that you could go your way . . . just doing your job and trying to get better at it without any feelings of covetousness . . .and the coveters (your company or your wife) would misconstrue your performance as "ambition"—which they would applaud. Or, if you have enough cool and a good enough sense of humor, you could slow down that covetousness of theirs without really challenging it. After all, if you challenge it (as covetousness), you're being the judge of their motives. And you could be wrong. The Leo-Christian, I think, ought to stick to judging his own motives and actions.

It's hard to imagine a LEO that doesn't covet.

It sure is.

And, this commandment probably covers a whole area of marketing that I sometimes wonder about . . . something we might get nailed for . . . when St. Peter questions us at the Pearly Gates.

What's that?

Well, *causing* covetousness in others. Promoting

and advertising products in ways that make people want things they can't afford, things they see (on TV) that "others have." We are aware of making children want things so badly that there are regulations against how directly you can appeal to their coveting impulses; but I wonder if adults are any better prepared to deal with this situation.

You are proposing that the government . . . or somebody . . . appoint itself the watchdog of these appeals to someone's tendency to covet?

No, I don't. I am really for business monitoring itself. If business shows that it is irresponsible, if it is using either money or psychological devices as weapons, I guess something has to be done to stop or slow their assault. But what I'm talking about is me . . . the individual Leo-Christian; it is I who must be my watchdog, to be sure that my "marketing" or "advertising" or "selling" efforts are not causing covetousness, not fostering people's greed or jealousy.

It may sound easy to avoid. With certain products, it's very hard to sell them **without** doing exactly that.

And could it be covetousness that causes big business conglomerates to take our businesses that don't want to be taken over?

In my view, being a proprietor is good but being a profiteer is bad.

To me proprietorship is running a business you're good at. You care about your craft and about your customers; you want to produce good stuff at a price the buyers are happy to pay—and you earn enough to pay your workers well and yourself well. It means being in THAT PARTICULAR business primarily because that's what you're good at—not primarily because of the monetary considerations.

To me, profiteering is being in a business primarily because you can make money at it—the more the better—and it doesn't matter to you whether it's a shoe factory or a pizza parlor.

Now, let's say a proprietor is running a good business—with happy employees and customers—and is satisfied with his profits, even though he is aware he could raise prices and make more profit. These days he is ripe for the coveter/profiteer. The way things are, a coveter/profiteer—aware that he could take over and make the extra profit the proprietor isn't making—can, with enough money, take over the proprietor's business, especially if it's a publicly-held corporation.

In this chapter, I'm not making the point that I feel sorry for the proprietor. (I do, but that's not the point.) I am concerned more about the motivation of the profiteer. How could he covet the profits from somebody else's business? Perhaps a business he even hates. Sad? Mad?

You are the one who is crazy. What you have just described is free enterprise under the capitalistic system. Are you a socialist?

Now it's time for YOU to "knock it off." I am not talking about free enterprise and capitalism vs socialism. NONE of them will work—as socialism certainly has proved—if individual people or groups take advantage of others.

You will never meet a more staunch advocate of free enterprise than I am. But it takes "good will toward men" to work.

And I am not comparing political systems at all. It's still Lion vs Christian under *any* political system you find in the world.

I am discussing me, really. I am asking myself:

Could I be a profiteer if I had the chance to take over a proprietor? Would I at least covet his profit?

I also admit that I worry about covetousness in all of us. It could wreck us as a nation and as a people.

But sometimes you're a victim of circumstance. You find yourself part of a movement. You get swept up in it—company covetousness—and you have no choice.

A Leo-Christian always has a choice. It's a question of whether we're up to it as individuals. No corporation I know of is destined to go to either heaven or hell en masse.

11

Christian Ethics vs Catholic Ethics
vs Protestant Ethics vs Jewish Ethics
vs Moslem Ethics vs Agnostic Ethics
vs Good Business and Productivity

I thought you said you weren't a theologian. Just how do you propose to tackle this chapter?

Actually, I don't. I just thought it was a nifty title. But I do think it makes me realize that I really can't judge for anyone but me. I have worked with Catholics, Lutherans, Jews, Moslems, agnostics, Buddhists, Mormons, Methodists, Baptists . . . people from 25 different countries speaking every imaginable language. I wish I could tell you that the Christians stood out from the others, that the Americans stood out from the others. But they didn't.

Only individuals did.

I didn't see any ruthless companies. Or Christian companies. I saw "good" people in all of them and "stinkers" in all of them . . . and of course, I am appointing myself as a committee of one to make that judgment, which is ridiculous in the first place.

I mean only to dramatize that the Leo-Christian dilemma is my dilemma. I must settle it for myself . . . but it is not a one-time commitment. It is a decision to be made each time the situation presents my Leo-Christian with a conflict.

If I feel that sex appeal will sell this product, shall I use sex appeal? If I feel that advertising on such-and-such a TV show will sell my product . . . but I think the show itself is immoral . . . do I do it? If I feel that built-in obsolescence is wrong, but profitable, do I opt for obsolescence? If I feel that mechanization will increase efficiency but put people out of jobs, do I mechanize?

If I am offered a job that I know will require me to "cheat a little" or "lie a little" . . . even if it's standard operating procedure in the Corporate Arena . . . do I take it?

If I own stock in a company that is making abortion implements . . . and I believe that abortion is a sin . . . do I keep my stock because it's paying marvelous dividends?

If I am a clergyman and know that talking about business sins from the pulpit might make my wealthier parishioners angry . . . do I do it anyway? If I am a businessman and I know that bringing religious or socially conscious considerations into business discussions may make my business associates angry . . . do I do it anyway?

If I preach (in private life) against cigarettes, liquor, status-symbol products, environment-destroying products, sugar products, or cosmetic products . . . is it okay to be in the business of manufacturing or selling them . . . as executive or clerk?

110

Is it okay to limit my Christian commitment in business to what's "legal" and what's "ethical"?

Do I have an obligation as a Leo-Christian not just to avoid sin . . . not break the commandments . . . but also to witness, to give an example, to spread Christ's word and love **at work?**

Can a Leo-Christian be a success as a Leo and a success as a Christian?

I hope so.

We needn't just hope so. We know so. That's what's beautiful. Notice the people at work who have drive—but the right kind of drive. They are eager to do *more* than the employer or customer asks . . . they serve those over them, under them, around them—and do it with a smile.

They bad-mouth nobody—not even competitors. They begrudge nobody—not even those who get paid more for less work.

They seek success, sales, profit, new business, victory—with spinnaker out and full-speed ahead—but never with malice or danger to life itself. It's a race, but only a race.

Sometimes, surely—I have no doubt—these "fools" are paid less than wheels which squeak louder, threaten more, and demand more.

They may miss out on a few shoddy perqs that—if offered—require that you already have a reputation for "going along with that sort of thing."

They may, to be blunt, not reach **as** high on the corporate ladder as they would if they were pushier and **would** "compromise" a little. But good Lions still rise to the top—even if they are Leo-Christians. And stay there longer than most.

They are mightily successful as Leos. They live in nice houses, their kids are well-fed, they sleep at night. They fear not the IRS, the CIA, or the PTA. But

111

more than that: **They love their work**—not just the paydays or reaching the next rung up the Corporate Ladder.

And they are mightily successful as Christians—because they GIVE WITNESS that He, too, works in the Corporate Arena. I have a hunch that God has a special place in His heart for Leo-Christians who "make it big" in commerce and industry.

It ain't easy.

Who said it was?

Me-The-Lion
vs
Me-The-Christian

I've been sitting here wondering why I chose to write this book in this format: with me-the-Lion (*in this style of type*) debating me-the-Christian (in this style of type).

Are there really *two of me* inside of me, struggling toward opposite goals, trying to serve two masters? Are Business and Christianity theoretically incompatible? Is it inevitable that my business life presents a conflict of Leo vs Christian, of Evil vs Good?

I am inclined to protest, to shout "NO!" at the top of my lungs. I want to say that I'm just like Joseph the carpenter of Nazareth, doing my work in praise of the Lord. And it's very true that I *don't* go through the day torn between a choice of Fame & Fortune vs My Christian Commitment . . . that I *do* feel that my Work Commitment and my Christian Commitment are thoroughly and mutually compatible. I can truly remember only a few instances in my life when I felt a conflict, felt confronted with a choice. And I can honestly say that the people and companies with whom I have worked have been highly ethical and have never asked me to do something patently crooked or immoral.

114

On the surface, my Leo and my Christian have worked together in such beautiful and serene harmony that I could almost conclude that *for me* . . . it's a breeze . . . so easy I hardly ever think about it.

And that's the problem: I hardly ever think about it.

But when I do . . . as I told myself at the beginning of this book . . . it's not enough to keep out of jail and keep the letter of the "don't" Commandments. It's not enough to "not sin" in obvious ways.

The real measure is whether I put out for Jesus as diligently as I put out for my company or my career . . . if I *strive to excel* as a Christian as much as I strive to excel as a Leo.

As a Leo . . . in my work . . . I am a hard worker. I expect of myself nothing but perfection; I work overtime to get it done and done right, with no thought of extra pay for my dedication; I would never just "put in my hours" or try to get by with the minimum. I am happy, enthusiastic, eager to learn more and get better; this year's performance must be *better* than last year's and I will knock myself out to make it so. I am a real Leo, success-oriented to the nth degree.

As a Christian . . . in my work . . . I am not like that at all. I make almost *no* conscious effort to "be Christian"; if Jesus came to see me at the office, He'd have to make an appointment . . . because I'm *so* busy. I seldom ask God for guidance in handling a delicate matter with an employee who has goofed up or we have decided to fire; nor do I thank Him for my talent, for my steady employment, for my raise or bonus. For even having a *job*. I try, but fail, to see others I work for and with as brothers and sisters loved and redeemed by Christ . . . or even *really* as people. I see them as cogs in the corporate machine, as trophies to be won in the race, as hurdles to be jumped or obstacles to be removed from the path of corporate progress. Oh, I realize that they have names. But do they have families? Feelings? Fears? Needs? Or hurts I could heal, if I'd notice?

We speak of the business world . . . the Corporate Arena . . . as a rat race, a jungle, cut-throat competition. And it can be.

But need it be? With God's help, it could be a glorious place for us to fulfill our Christian commitment—especially for Leo types who have enthusiasm, drive, talent, leadership. We are the ones people notice, perhaps look up to . . . whose Christ-witness, smiles, thoughtfulness, unselfishness, peace, and spirit could brighten a whole office building or factory or store . . . brighter than the electric company can.

With God's help, I said. And I confess that I haven't often asked for it . . . and by "it" I mean specifically, help to become the Leo-Christian I could be.

And so, to express that need, I have written a Leo-Christian Daily Prayer. I wrote it for me; but I offer it to you and to Leo-Christians everywhere . . . if you'd like to use it.

May we meet in heaven. If we do, I hope we can talk business . . . because I really *do* love it.

Thanks for listening!
Wally

A LEO-CHRISTIAN DAILY PRAYER

Lord, I need You . . . especially from 9 to 5.

FATHER, I need You to keep reminding me that Your business is a lot more important than my business. That You are the only real Big Shot, my only permanent Employer. Keep my eye on the only bottom line that counts: Yours. Give me the faith and the guts to pass up (or rebel against, when necessary) anything that is good for my business but bad for Yours. Like Solomon, I ask You for an understanding heart, to deal with people the way You would want me to.

JESUS, I need You to remind me that even though I'm part of management, I still belong to a union: the brotherhood of Christ. To which I must pay my dues. I need You to remind me that competitors, fellow employees, suppliers, and customers are people You love as much as You love me and that I am supposed to do likewise. Show me (for I am blind) the many opportunities I have each day to let people see You through me. If I ever get greedy, please throw my money changer out of my temple. If I ever try to "win by intimidation" please make me lose.

HOLY SPIRIT, I need You to come to work with me every day. Remind me to wonder why other people . . . many of whom work at menial tasks or carry heavy loads but whose work is of more service to mankind . . . make less money than I do. Please hold my hand when I make out my income tax and my expense report. Please hold my arm when I am tempted to pat myself on the back; I need humility, not more praise.

LORD, I also thank You. I thank You for granting me whatever talent I have for the business I'm in . . . and for enjoying my work. Remind me to treat it as sacred, as a vocation, as a means to fulfill my Christian commitment . . . not as a separate island of my life. Most of all, Lord, remind me that I *am* baptized . . . not "was" baptized . . . every minute of every day, especially from 9 to 5.

LORD, help me be a success—by *Your* standards. Bless me. Inspire me. Use me. Turn me on.